The Three Keys to Spiritual Awareness

The First Key: The Human Body

Author Maha Ete

Index

Introduction

For the last year, while on the internet, I have used the term "the three keys". I found these individual elements over 50 years of research and practice. The search began in my twenties and is still ongoing. Indeed, initially, as separate elements, they much later became interlocked. Yes, we have three individual spiritual affecting components inside each of us.

Exploring and using these individually and together during my spiritual development was valuable and necessary to gain an understanding of myself. Initially, for more than several decades, it was singular. Slowly as I found more, I began incorporating more. Each became my focus, from the initial book research then progressing to human training. With the basics in hand, I continued with years of experimentation and practice to that element's culmination. Once completed, I then shifted to the next one when guided to.

Admittedly, it has taken me 50-odd years to explore, test, develop, retest, and prove each and assess their efficacy. Only in the last decade did I begin to see how the individual elements bonded into a skill set with the ability sometimes to combine the three on the people I was healing.

The methods were learned firstly as a Buddhist, then as a spiritualist, and finally, Sha man (not a shaman). I have used and am using the three keys to open myself. Because of this exploration and the methods learned and abilities found, I hopefully healed others to varying degrees. Initially, to a lesser degree and over time, I became more proficient as I acquired greater skills, training in their usage, then refining each and melding them into an overall approach.

My journey started with chasing for an explanation regarding the energy I had flowing within me by asking two Roman Catholic priests. It turned out they were useless and knew nothing about it. They thought I was delusional. I then resorted to book learning to find different answers for it.

I found nothing initially because there was not much around in the mid to late 60s and 70s, so I studied several meditation methods instead. While using these, it not only led to a handful of heightened awareness, super-conscious states, but this practice also increased the flow, strangely by silencing the mind.

During one of these heightened awareness states, I saw a Native American in a headdress, which made me switch from Buddhism to spiritualism and its healing, empathy, and intuition training practices.

Admittedly this was the closest practice in the West, resembling both Christ's way, the tribal shamanic ones and the East's energy usage. It also was the closest I came to explaining and using the energy I had inside me.

This Spiritualist methodology made me see that energy was transferable between spirit and people through the medium of a healer. This transferred energy was of a higher pitch than the energy moving up my spine.

I, decades on, reached a ceiling point with spiritualist practices. Then because of internal infighting, I branched out again into several shamanic, tribal introspection, visualisations, and practises, i.e., symbolic magic, the animal mind, and animal spirit synergy. I saw the similarity between western and shamanic practises regards the mind and tied many of the concepts and practises together.

So, in hindsight, this is not how this series is structured; however, everyone is guided onto their path via different methods. Energy flows led to meditation practises, healing people, proving spirits exist, other ESP experiences, and my body. These were my order.

After half a century, the once initially singular usage on self and others has progressed; to where they are a blend of all three, or individually as required—my intuitive skills determine whether individual, two or three methods are used.

I start the series where we all begin in this life in the physical body.

Chapter one: Conception, pre-birth and birth.

I'm starting from our time in the physical when we are conceived in our mother's womb. Our biological life begins from the first second sperm joins the egg. We are acting and reacting to the input and stimuli around us. This physical only interaction continues for several months before the spirit enters, and the body is referred to as a whole.

I suppose we can say we exist when I or recognition of self can be recorded and felt, and spirit can communicate with the body component now joined and living.

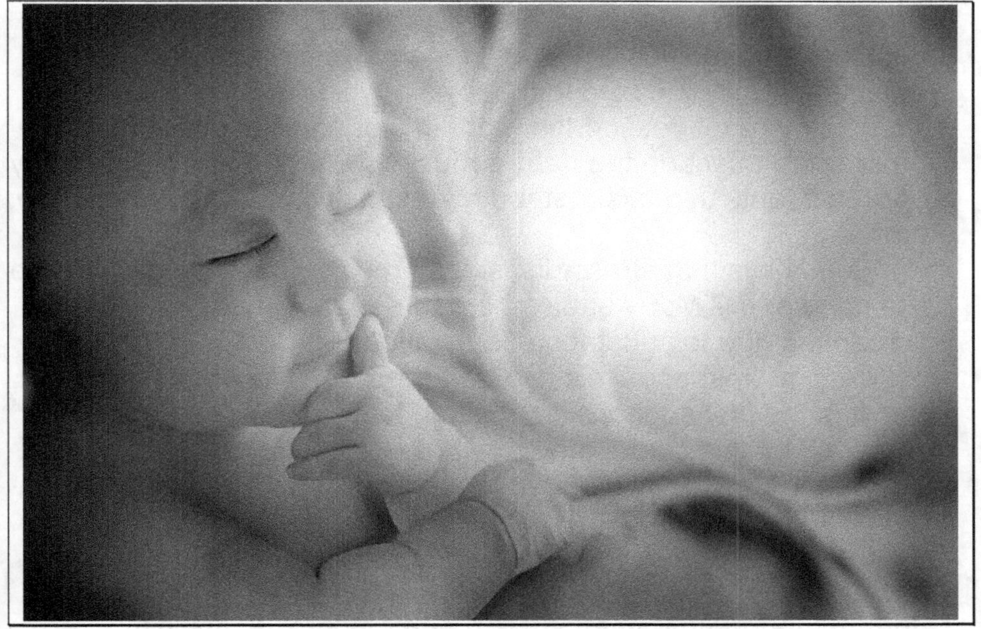

For the next six odd months, we are still considered totally in the reactive mind state. As our mind and awareness increase, we take in increasingly more of mum's mental and physical health state. Externals also, e.g., sound from the external world as we develop further.

On the very cellular level, we can feel the changes in what mum's feeling by our reactions to the hormones in the food supply. However, it is not just hormonal communication in the womb, float tank; we have an extended psychic, telepathic, and empathic awareness of our mothers.

As both body and mind develop cognitive thinking, assessment and feedback up the line to mum happens. Women's urges for specific foods could very well be communications from the foetus to the mother based on the child's growing body's requirements.

I would go as far as to postulate some people's hate of their mothers starts in the womb and begins due to the mother's feeling toward the lump in her belly. Many mothers' addictions flow on effects to the unborn baby also.

The problem with cognitive function is that it makes the foetus open to negative feedback. So, mum's wild hormonal, habit or substance abuse flow-on effects and psychological shifts get reflected into and locked in a baby's physical muscular self.

The more distressed the mother is during her pregnancy, the greater the effect on the baby's musculature. I suspect that many unborn infants use this method to desensitise themselves before birth.

Hey, if it is that stressful inside of mum, what the hell will it be like once born? Many babies born to addicted mothers are born screaming due to substance deprivation.

In some respects, this can be called the sins of the mother, and it is the first subconscious dump if the child is too over-whelmed by this tide of emotion, both theirs and mum.

During one of my meditation sessions, I accessed a pre-birth memory of happily floating in a warm place.

I don't remember the birth, and the only physical aspect of post-birth was that because I had been born fully aware of spirit, energy, and matter, what I saw made me lock muscles in my thighs, forearms, neck, around the eyes, distorting the left side more than the right also creating a distortion between left hand and right-hand sides of both body and mind shortly after birth.

A vague recollection of the priest baptising me completed the physical-only neutering of spiritual abilities as he was, in today's terminology, a war criminal hiding behind the church's mask. My father had fought with the Italian partisans and was captured and coerced into forced labour in Germany. His pain was hard to look at, also.

Recently my forays into scrying the future have awakened multiple kriyas and pullbacks in pain from the visions accessed. So, a bit of both the pain in others and the pain from seeing future events locked me back into just the typical human awareness pattern.

At this stage, I was unaware of any distortions in my musculature or sight ability.

Chapter 2: Preteen recollections

Further body Armouring occurred around age six.

Possibility one: as a migrant, my family were housed at the Bonnegila camp. I vaguely recall hiding under one of the upraised wooden buildings from something. Second alternative: I recollect walking down a deserted road, clothes dishevelled well after preschool had finished. The only highlight of that walk was finding coloured pencils on the sidewalk. What happened prior still eludes me.

After moving from Norwood, I was obsessively self-conscious about not being noticed, even starting to hide when others were picked to do the twist in class. I was unsure if the teacher saw me cringing away as I was not picked.

This need not to be noticed or speak about it; I believe it caused me to have severe long-term tonsillitis infections around age 6-7 until surgical removal.

Other recollections regarding the first two years of primary school were that I was comfortable and made friends with a wide range of nationalities. At the same time, I kept away from joining a cultural gang or fighting out the back of the school and even hid once in 2nd-year primary school, trying not to get involved.

I suspect this was my first physical flow-on effect from my subconscious trauma in my early years.

Chapter 3:Reconnecting to my body 40s and on

I had an everyday migrant life with average school results in all, but physical education, which I am sure was still being hindered by the don't excel or be noticed edict. I say this because the one time I didn't think about doing the long jump and just did it, I surprised everyone, including myself and landed in the top length range for my group. The next jump, I fudged it again and fell backwards. Where I had landed was well behind the first attempt.

I will skip the marriage, have kids and family, get divorced part of my life, and get to where my body started to get involved in the release process.

As mentioned, the first indications were medical, with severe tonsilitis reinfections a few years after migrating to Australia requiring removal. This illness was followed in my forties by a saliva stone that kept getting reinfected, one gallstone on the first ultrasound, and a second detected on the following scan a decade or more later.

Self-assessment had me find and then know that both vertical neck and right-hand thigh muscles were in lockdown from around age 40, with the thigh one producing the more varied effects. At times it would alternate from feeling intensely cold to burning hot temperature-wise when I got older.

To the touch, it stood and still stands out when massaged compared to the other leg muscles as a knotted muscle length from the knee to upper thigh and has been painful over several levels over the decades when massaged.

Some ten years later, the following muscles awakened mainly during meditation. These include starting from the top of the head down, tremors in muscles around the eyes, REM-type movement in and around the eyes, L.H. cheek extension back towards the ear, and tension in the chin area. The lower jaw is introverted, i.e., pulled back from the upper. In the chest, noticeable shoulder drops, re-tenses upwards and further drops, shoulder blade flexes and clicks during the more reactive flexes during the last year's meditation sessions. Just below the rib cage, both heat and flexing in the lateral stomach muscles below the ribs and just flexing in the vertical L.H. ones. Upper arms only recently began showing mild pain during meditation. Legs barring the muscles mentioned so far have no indications.

Kriyas

The Wiki definition is "Kriyā (Sanskrit क्रयिा, "action, deed, effort") most commonly refers to a "completed action", technique or practice within a yoga discipline meant to achieve a specific result."

My definition is the attempt by the body to release locked-in body trauma via uncontrolled muscle tremors. Admittedly, this muscle shaking for me was brought about by doing meditation. So, a technique was used to get to a level of awareness of the muscular lockdown. They commenced releasing motions during the meditation when a steady mental awareness level was achieved, i.e. This after more than 20 years of introspection.

I beg to differ regarding the "completed action" as my kriyas haven't been completed in that they are merely stages of release, not complete release.

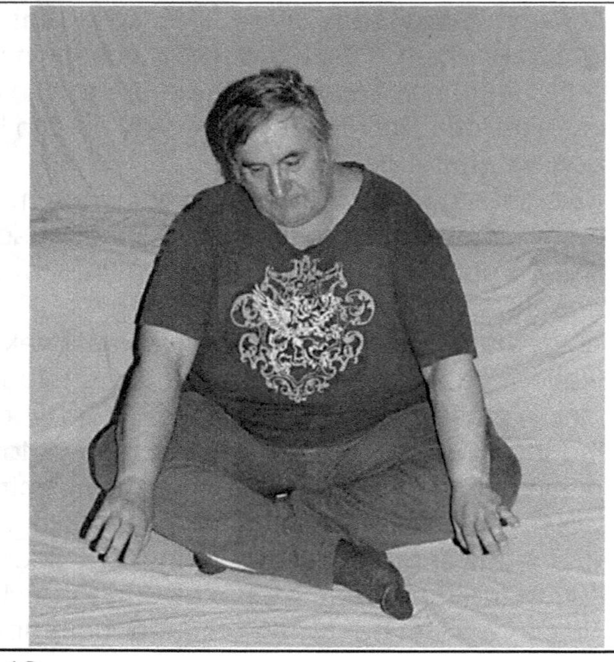

The picture above was taken after several minutes of meditating when my lateral stomach muscles began shaking and broke my semi-lotus thumb and finger mudra stance.

Two thousand twenty-two, these muscular contraction release moments also began occurring outside of the meditative state, mainly either before I fell asleep or just after waking. The fact this is occurring suggests the complete release is closer now.

The right-hand shoulder blade has become intensely painful for several months now, indicating my body is accelerating the release mechanism. Now in November, after three months of excruciating pain, if I stretched a certain way, the pain seems to have gone.

Chapter 4: The Body's Traumatic Indicators

Pain

Most of us have points on our bodies that react painfully when a slight to moderate amount of pressure is applied. When we are younger, these are no-shows and have no input in what we do or feel. As we grow older, similar failures in life can apply more pressure to the original muscle or organ affected and then, when sufficiently disturbed, emerge as myalgia or nerve pain until rectified.

The picture below shows that either an ice or heating pack can treat it. Dad and mum would heat a brick, wrap a towel around it and hold it on the pain. My friend used her hot water bottle on her stomach, which she found beneficial and soothing. I used acupuncture while others medicated.

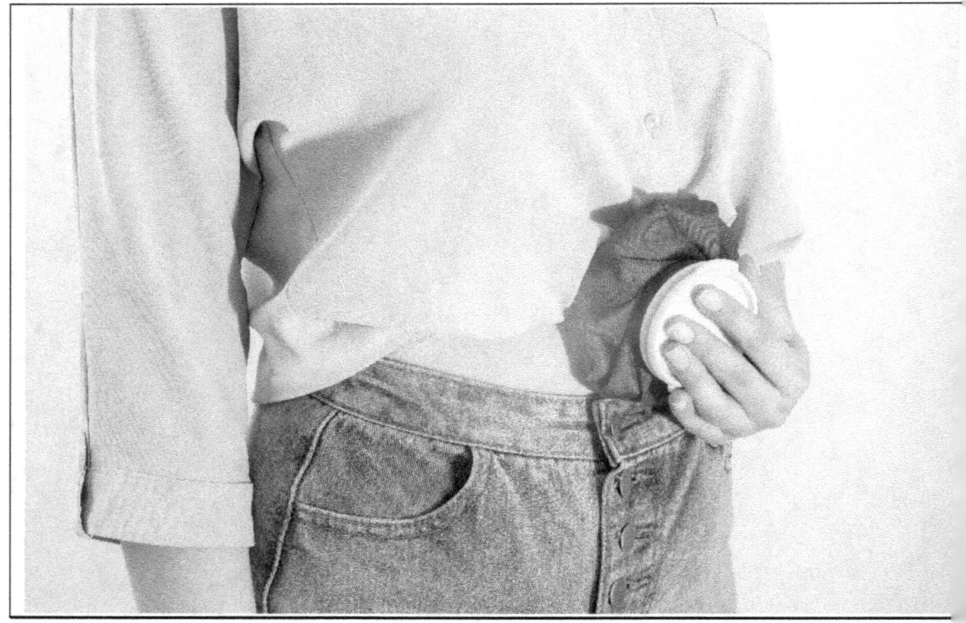

The second method is how trauma induces electrical current changes in our bodies. These can be found and partly fixed with acupuncture, electronic attached to needles or just needles alone and acupressure.

The third is by the body reacting and trying to shake the trauma out of itself with what the East calls kriyas.

Kriyas are involuntary muscle contraction release spasms often associated with devotees on the spiritual path.

Let me say this once, and once only kriyas, even those that scrunch one up into foetal positions, are not epilepsy. Why? Because the epileptic fit needs to finish on its own, whereas the kriyas, mild or extreme, can be stopped by yourself, or so I've discovered.

Secondly, they are most often initiated by meditative states, not nerve damage or short circuits in the brain.

Chapter 5: Historical remedial methods

For most, there wasn't much available other than herbal remedies, massages, and saunas. These methods, herbs, massage, and sauna, came and went depending on the stability in the area, with the more affluent partaking and benefitting the most. Records as below can be found in many countries and races' historical books. Herb remains have been found in the tombs of the Pharaohs.

Akmanthor in Egypt shows the practice of massage.

In the East, Hindus developed the ashram and retreat yogic system, which cut back to bare bones, was 1/3 scripture, 1/3 exercise and 1/3 meditation, and incorporating breathe work and yoga training.

Many yoga exercise routines today include keeping and maintaining a healthy body with muscle stretches, breathing and meditative relaxation.

The physical exercises made the body supple and healthy. Also, as the devotees had to find their meals, they spent quite some time walking and asking for alms and food several times per day.

Poses in yoga

At 71, I now potter around in the garden in my backyard and do some short walks.

The second part of yoga meditation relates more to the other keys.

I use a semi-lotus leg positioning, two separate mudras, the left-hand one above, with both hands resting on the knees. Uncertain if she's doing a breathing exercise at the same time.

The physical negatives of the above pose up until a few years back were squashed and numb toes, in one ankle much more than the other, requiring several minutes of stretching and massage to recover feeling or be capable of standing on. The other problem is I would and still do get severe cramping. The strange thing about the cramps is I can meditate them away. If one can get to a certain meditative depth, the pain disappears.

Tai Chi

Tai Chi and martial arts in the monasteries in China and Asia aimed to improve physical health and promote a self-defence and meditation style.

Offshoots into medicine also with both the acupuncture and acupressure techniques proliferating.

Tai Chi master

Shao Lin martial arts.

Sweat Lodges were used by the Norse and American Indians

American Indian sweat lodge.

Herbalism dates to prehistoric times. Although both my parents knew of and used herbal concoctions and teas and had a European culinary style, I haven't delved that much into herbs. Dad even brought an Italian herbal from Italy as a prized possession which he leant out and was never returned.

I read somewhere that the Roman Empire's soldiers didn't travel anywhere without garlic, and no, it wasn't garlic breath that won their empire, lol. It supposedly has anti-viral, anti-fungal properties and is good for skin, heart, and high blood pressure conditions.

The last large-scale use of herbs was in WW1 when the front's hospitals ran out of disinfectants and medicines. They used sphagnum moss in the West to help with sepsis and garlic as a salve after operations in Russia.

It was only in the last few years that I've resorted to stinging nettle tea for a prostate problem and found it quite helpful.

HERBS

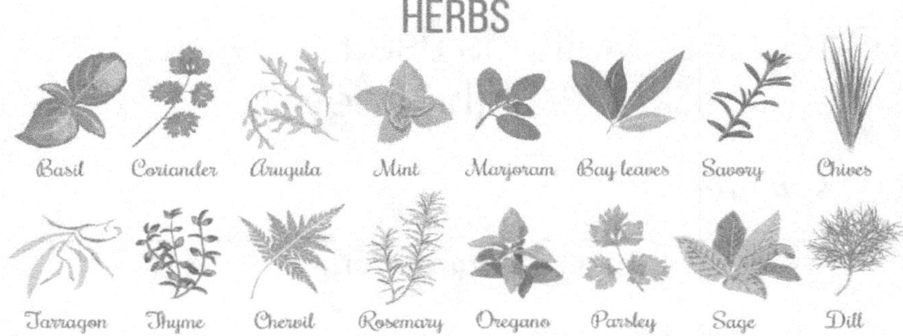

Many of the above herbs are both culinary and herbal. The main ones used as herbals by my parents were bay, mint, rosemary and sage. Culinary Rucola (arugula) as a salad, add chives in a scrambled egg frittata, parsley as a general all-over add-in, and rosemary chopped up fine as a garnish, general soup add-in, or cooked with steaks.

Chapter 6: Methods used to awaken and treat the body

Acupuncture

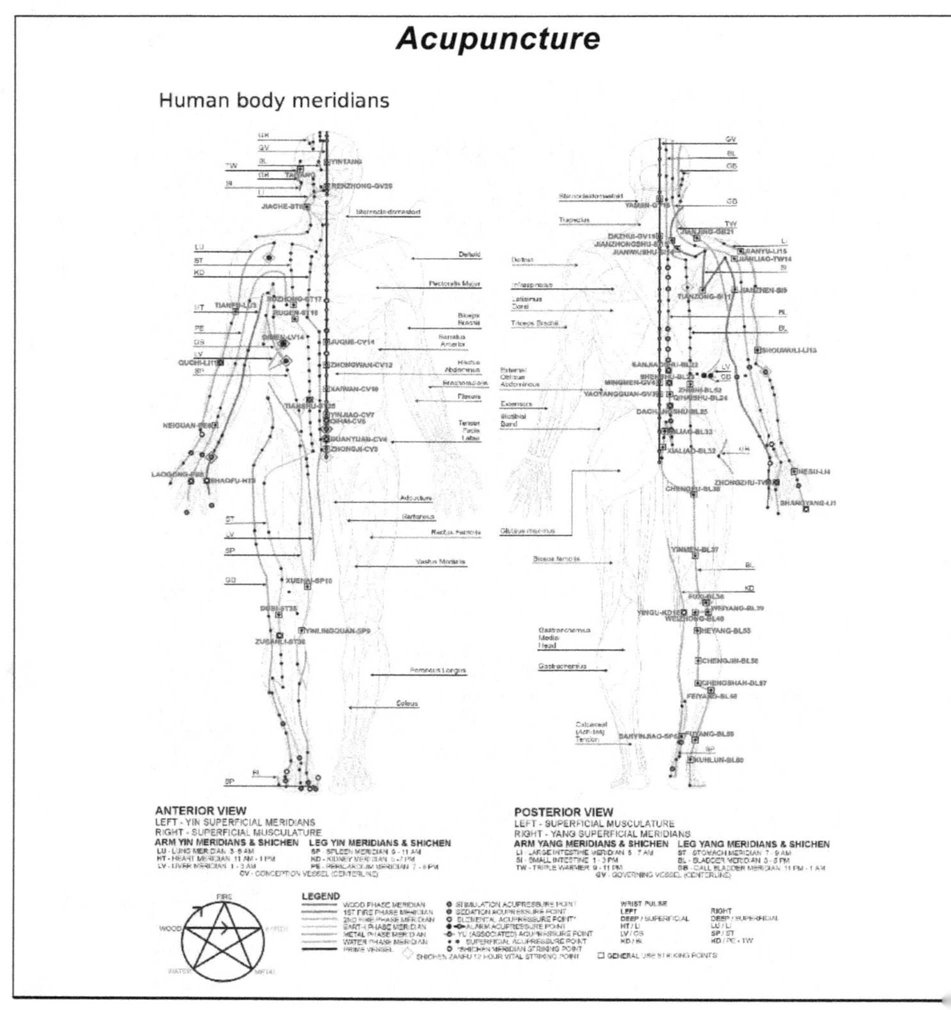

I tried and saw two different acupuncturists more than a decade apart. The first told me that acupuncture can release emotions and that he would treat me with Chinese herbs instead

I passed a few small kidney stones using them over several weeks, but no acupuncture.

In the second treatment, a husband-and-wife team used both acupuncture needles and then ran an electric current through them. I must admit, I didn't think I benefitted much from the two sessions I had with them, other than gaining more experience in feeling the effects on my body as they related to the age of the traumatic injury.

However, because of the comment made during my first visit, I bought a Slimnstim electronic acupuncture machine from Tandy. Admittedly most of its initial usage was on my father and his painful back issues. Its efficacy with his back pain had the machine need battery replacement every couple of years.

It was only later, during my 50s and 60s, that I began using it on myself. Admittedly, it was a time of experimentation and attempting to fast-track my spiritual development.

Experimenting, I utilised the search part of the machine and found where I required treatment by finding the points of electrical anomaly. When the beeper raised its pitch to high, I clicked the electronic component and zapped myself. The primary use later in life was to relieve my pain.

I suppose I should include a warning here as quite a few people I suggested and tried acupuncture on to relieve their pain opted out because of the pain. I suppose I have a higher pain threshold, for starters and can see the benefit of the short-term pain as compared to a day to days of pain relief with my neck and back after the car accidents.

Pain isn't the only response that the body gives when receiving electronic acupuncture. At worst, my knees gave out when experimenting in the shoulder blades area, and I started falling, which broke the connection and thus stopped my downward descent. Other reactions include—large areas of facial muscle tremors in the cheek, ear, neck, and shoulder regions.

Although I found temporary alleviation of neck soreness and the beeper response level dropped after several days of consecutive usage, as did the muscle tremors, it was only a temporary fix to the muscular problems. They would return sometime later and required retreatment.

For myself, I kept the settings on maximum. For others, I adjusted them to what they could stand when they let me use the machine.

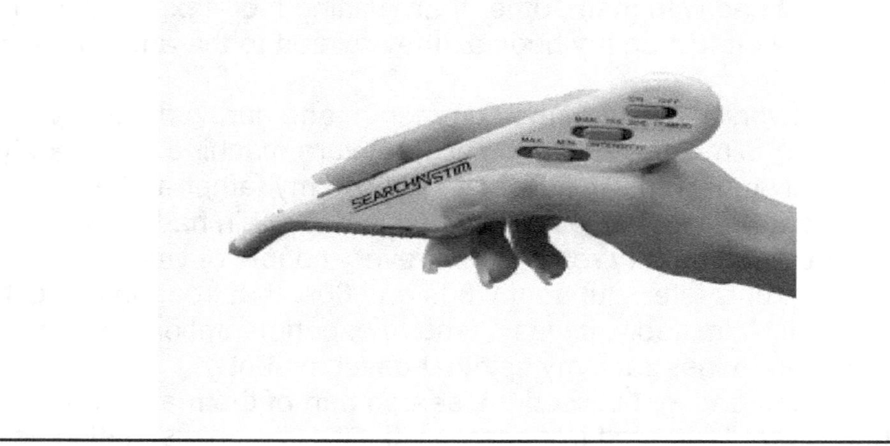

So, although valid for short-term pain relief, the acupuncture I performed on myself overall had little to no effect on the longer-term muscle trauma locked in my system.

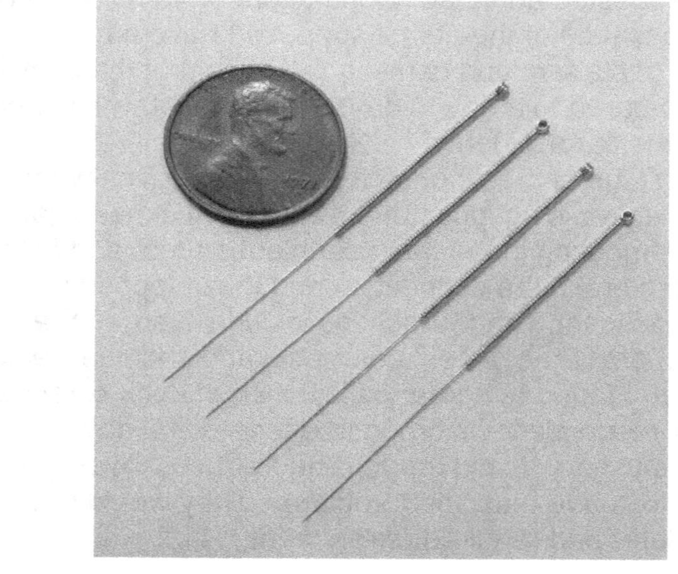

Acupuncture needles

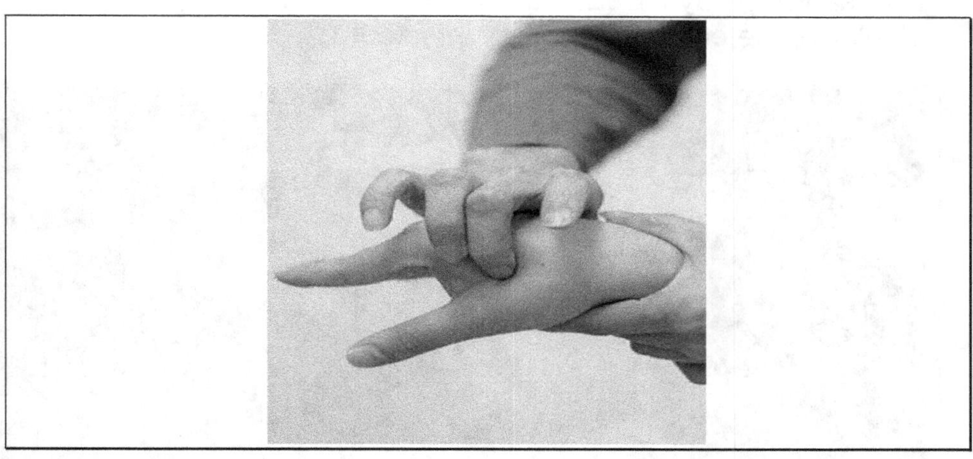

My usage on others, especially as I lost the searchnstim behind a cabinet for several years, was through the intuitive approach and then working on that single point with the middle index finger and around it with both thumb for a larger area and index fingers on the pain area, gently at first and then over weeks with a deeper massage.

Intuitively probing with my fingers into people's backs and other areas, even gently, has had several people uncontrollably jerk away from the finger, shouting "Ow", the pain felt vocally with even light to moderate pressure. The more I worked on those areas, the less the initial reaction happened. I did that to my daughter on 3/10/2022, thinking I didn't need to scan her, as I'd worked there before. I opted for the prod at moderate pressure and produced the "Ow, take it easy" reaction.

I have found this excessive response more applicable when life's trials and tribulations stress people. So yes, our muscles become tenser and more painful as stress increases.

Another Chinese method I haven't personally experienced, but a friend of mine swore by, is cupping. According to her, it released toxins in her body and left some bruising occasionally. Although there were a few instances of excessive bruising, I recall. My assessment that it shouldn't get that bad didn't dissuade her.

Although the photo below is of a cupping and blood-letting set, and I read somewhere that giving blood to the Red Cross occasionally has some benefits, I don't recommend it performed in unsanitary ways. Better to donate than, depending on the sterility of the equipment, to get infected.

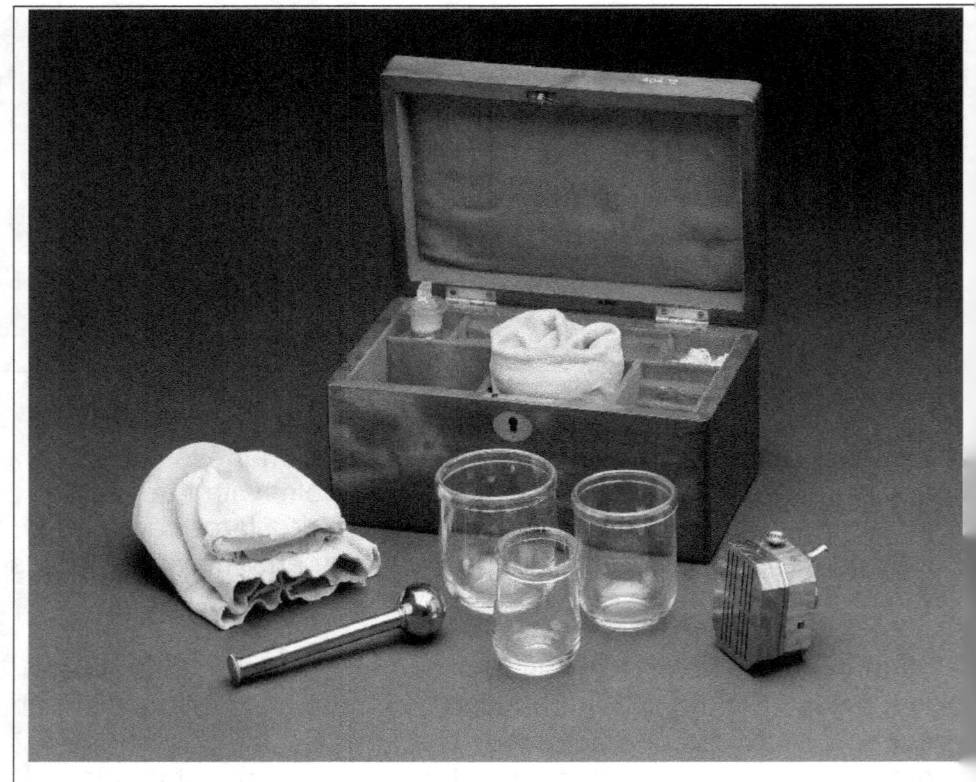

Old-time cupping and blood-letting set.

Moxibustion

Used frequently in Chinese and Asian films and series is a heat treatment that sometimes incorporates acupuncture points as the treatment area.

Physical Massage Techniques

Skeletal muscles

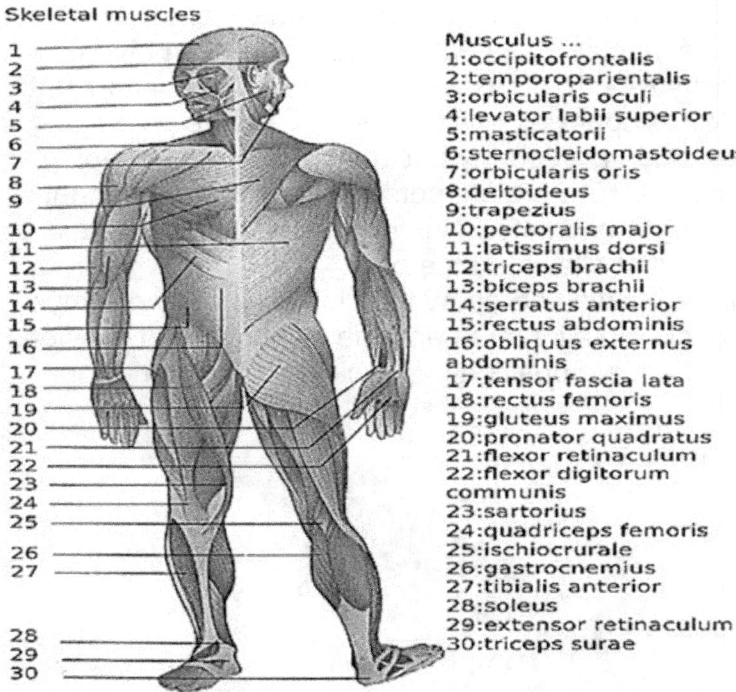

I was introduced to massage as a healing medium in the Spiritualist Church. Here we were instructed to do light massages, mainly on the shoulders.

Although most of my healing in the Spiritualist Church was of the energy transfer kind, I ensured that at the end of the healing, I would give their shoulders and arms a light hug and a "God bless you."

There were times only in the last few years when I did the pinch test on the neck and shoulder muscles to test stress levels before massaging, and where I found sufficient tightness, I provided light to moderate massage to that area.

I utilised several masseuses in my life using the following types of massage: Bowen (male), general overall (2 separate females), and Chinese (male) over some 30 years, so, not overly, although thinking I should often.

I performed most of my massage work on myself by using a heavy variable vibrating with a heat option machine. The manual self-type of massage was the next most used.

Chiropractic

My primary physical medical professionals were five chiropractors, especially post-car accidents, the first of which, because of his strength, didn't need the clickety-clack tool until later in life. After unpacking a widescreen T.V., the packaging started falling, and I cricked my back, stopping it from tipping. That was when my sure-fire chiropractor failed with the manual fix and started using an actuator. Unfortunately, the actuators didn't fix my problems just alleviated the pain.

The main areas worked on by the chiropractors were my neck, lower back, hip alignment and the last couple of sessions mid-chest via the table positioning, back cracking, and drop effect.

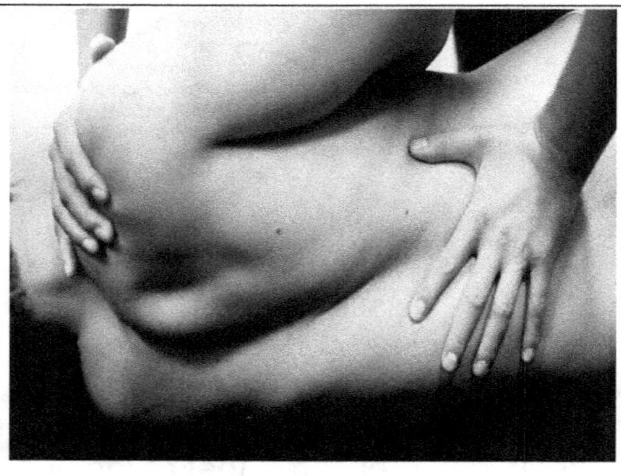

The twist and push spine manipulation

An actuator

An actuator: All the chiropractor's bar one used actuators on my spine and manual manipulation on my neck, elbow, and hips. On several occasions, they would use small pillow elevators in the hip region to adjust my lower back. One or two used heavy vibrators before the actuators.

BTW sitting on an overfilled wallet had thrown my hips out of alignment, so keep your wallets in your side pockets.

Rolfing and deep tissue massage

Unfortunately, I haven't had the experience and have never needed or had to get that deep or had the finger strength to do this massage technique, even though some people would swear I did. However, the initial pain-filled deep tissue type of massage seems to have been modified.

Chapter 7: My Massaging Techniques

The massaging for me became used more as a healer with a lady, at first girlfriend, and shortly after full-time rescue. Admittedly the massage and acupressure worked better on her than I had ever imagined. The benefits, however, were enhanced by simultaneously using other techniques in conjunction with the massage.

One of the reasons that it worked so well was the intensive twice and sometimes three times weekly half-hour massage sessions. The efficacy of this intensive massage I assessed by the pinch test. Muscles decreased in their tightness over many months from hard to normal. And, yes, it took months to destress her in her mid-fifties.

The areas of primary attention were the upper arms with both the push-down and flow-style motion massage, both vertically and laterally across the muscles. There was also the scrunch, where I would stretch and compress the muscles with the fingers and then let go and rinse, repeating across the total area massaged.

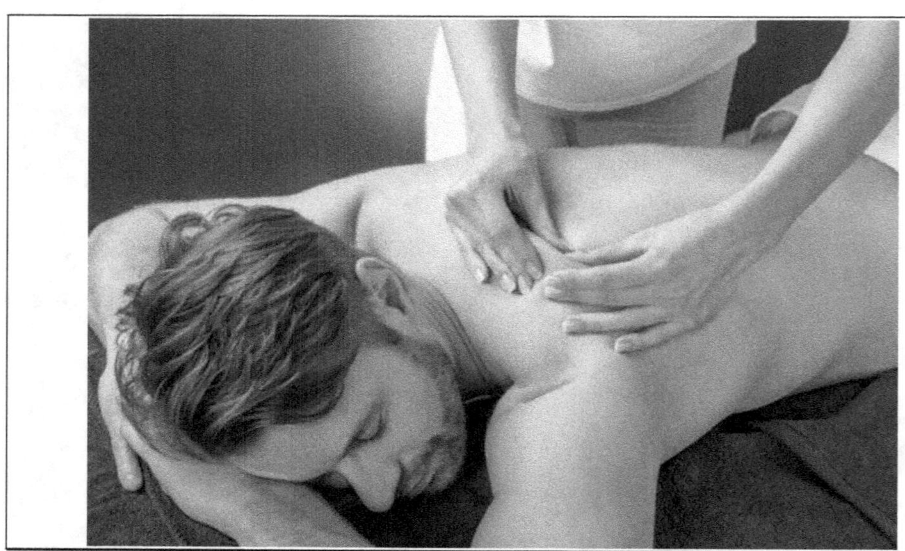

The areas on the body where I used this on myself were on the lower arm, drawing the flesh inwards in between the two bones from wrist to elbow, on my right-hand thigh, working from just above the knee up to the thigh along my frozen muscle, lower R.H. front of the leg.

Another massage technique: wrap the hand around the forearms and massage down from the elbow to the wrist back and forth in a twisting motion.

A variation is with the palm flat curving it around the shoulder blade. I worked the thumb and or side of the palm over the muscles. I worked on the shoulder blade curvature, firmly pushing the hand area around the shoulder blade bone.

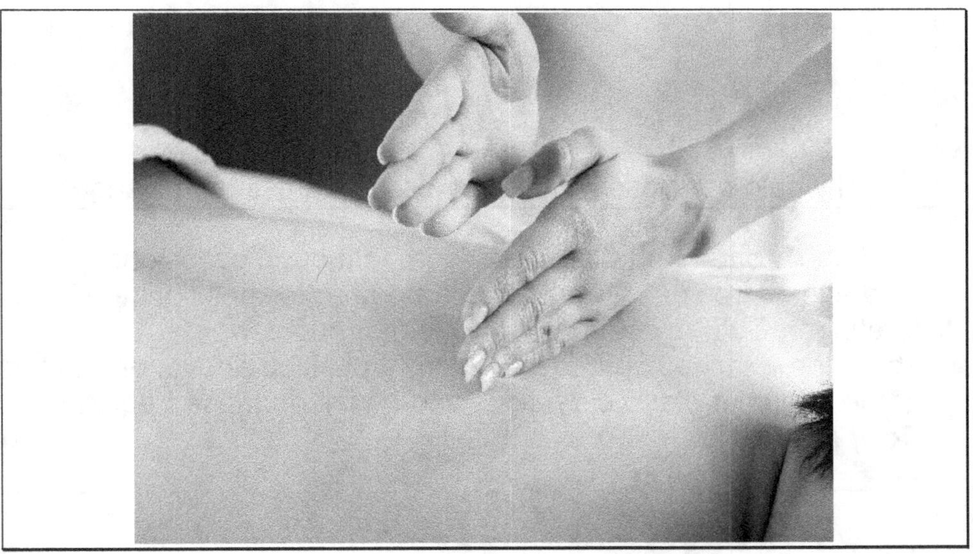

Drumming: moving the vertical palm, as per above, over the spine and larger muscled areas. The other main fingers massage is, instead of fingers closed as above, wide open to start the strike. With the next hit, move the hand slightly up the muscle or area consecutively with repeat open finger striking in one percussive vibrating pattern and repeat. So instead of just one hit, you get a repeated, percussive hit as each finger contacts the prior.

These percussion-type massages have proven amazingly effective in healing soft tissue injuries.

The prod or poke and slight circular swirl in the pain area were not used on myself. I used these primarily on others to produce reliable results combined with a deep breathing technique.

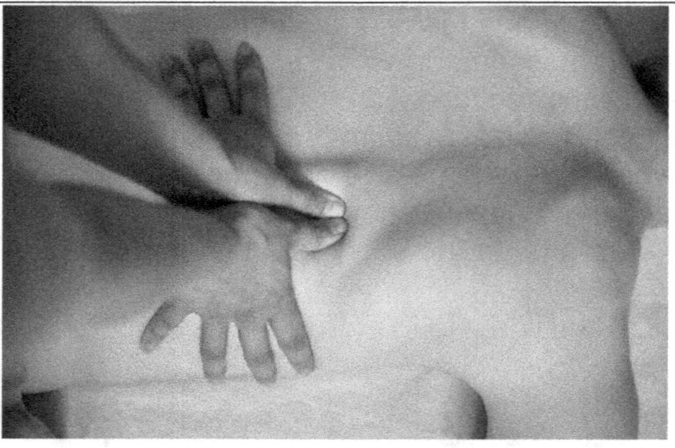

I would not classify the above as deep-tissue massage.

I use a one-hand thumb pressure, although occasionally, where less pressure is required or the area is specific, the forefinger. Both my daughter and granddaughter have knots about three inches up from the current position above, on the top of the shoulder blade curvature, and I work on these frequently.
Foot massages

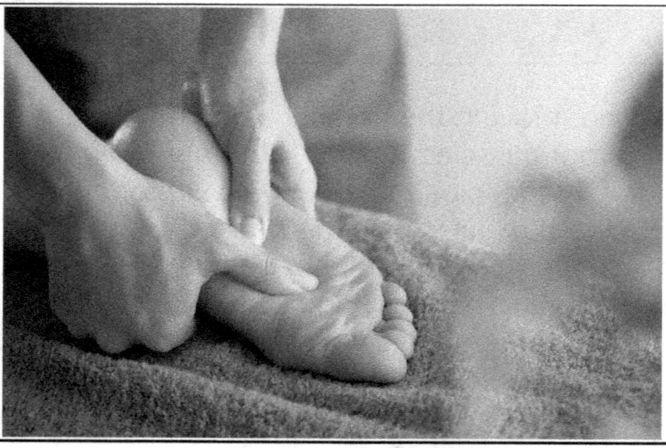

My foot massages have been appreciated by many women lovers and others that I gave them to because of the relaxing, pleasurable qualities.

The technique varies. The single thumb pressing move above on individual foot spots is one—the thumb flowing over the foot's inner curvature from toe to heel. The heel grasp, rotate and massage. The top of the foot: lightly massage between the bones down to the toes—the gentle squeezing and manipulation of individual toes to finish.

Another is tugging the sides of the foot to widen it slightly and then slightly compress it.
I used a slightly scented massage oil with both rosemary and sandalwood fragrances.

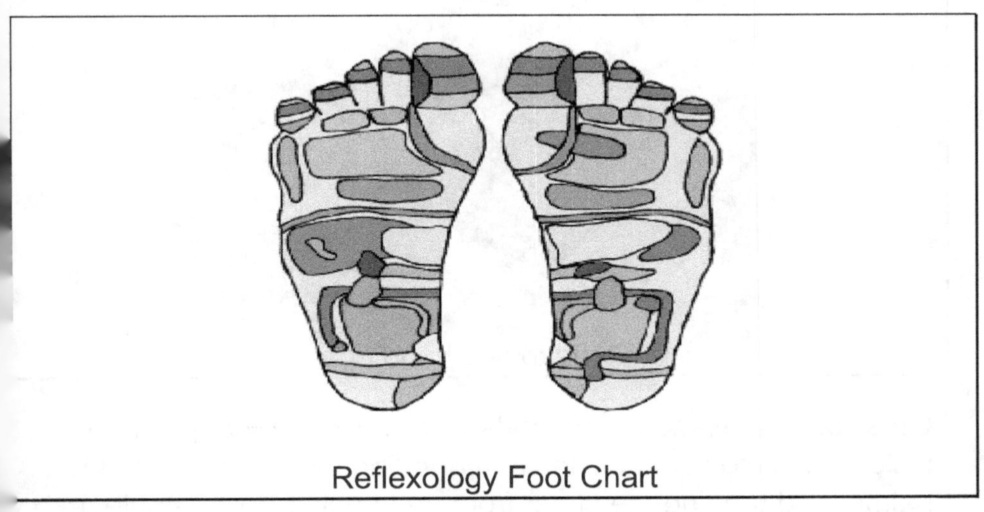
Reflexology Foot Chart

I went to a psychic fair 30 years ago and met the head of the Reflexology practice here in South Australia. I volunteered to be a guinea pig in the lecture. The chiropractor who I visited the most had also trained in this field and took on the mantle of head of that organisation later, occasionally using this technique on me.

His findings were: I had problems with Number 2's and that after I went home, I should press the area in my crotch and expect fast results. That problem poop retention had been one in early childhood, so I was unsure of his diagnosis as I did not feel it was still a problem.

The other area mentioned was the fleshy bit between the thumb and the first finger.

He also used my palm wave, an energy movement healing technique. Reflexology is a blend of massage and energy movement.

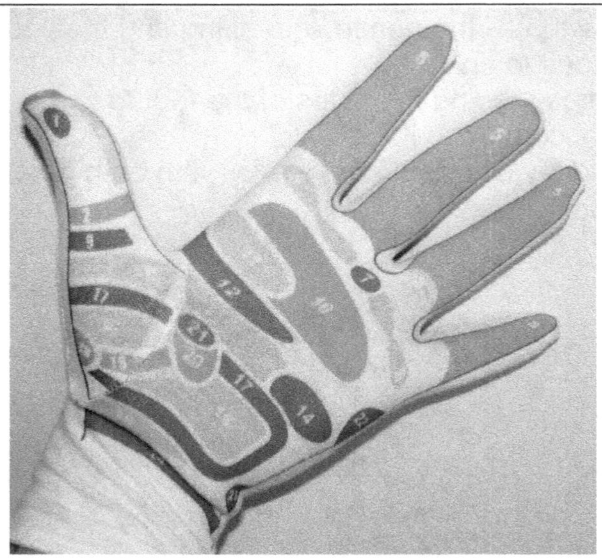

Reflexology hand chart

Other body massaging methods I have used and applied included: using my knuckles in a grinding motion, cupping the palms, and tapping the chest front and back to relieve phlegm; and as a percussion type massage, the elbow for deep-seated muscle tension and to assist with hand strain.

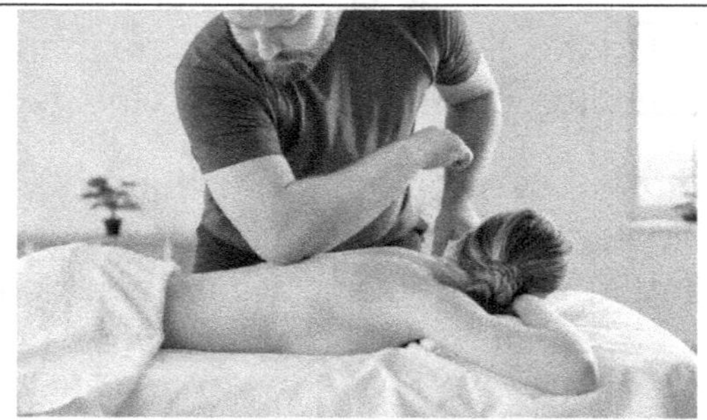

I have heard of walking on the back as a Japanese method, but I am not experienced in this, nor have I found someone sufficiently light or experienced enough to do it on me.

Temporary and long-term massage techniques.

Most of the time, manipulative massaging, acupuncture, and acupressure will only provide temporary and often relaxing pleasurable health benefits. The pain resurfaces and requires reapplication when the underlying causes resurface for whatever reason when life knocks us again.

There is some evidence that long-term, several sessions per week can destress the body to a point where the day-to-day grind can be managed and coped with for quite some time after the end of the sessions.

However, ample evidence was found where abnormal stresses will return the prior stress, and associated emotional symptoms should one cease receiving them before finding the initial cause.

Lymphatic Drainage

"Manual lymphatic drainage (MLD) is a type of massage based on the hypothesis that it will encourage the natural drainage of the lymph, which carries waste products away from the tissues back toward the heart"

Although most of my massage techniques could be classified as this, I only considered this as I worked on people's feet with this flow, lymph-clearing technique.

Craniosacral Therapy

"Craniosacral therapy (CST) or cranial osteopathy is a form of alternative therapy that uses gentle touch to palpate the synarthrodial joints of the cranium. CST is a pseudoscience, and its practice has been characterised as quackery.[1][2] It is based on fundamental misconceptions about the physiology of the human skull and is promoted as a cure-all for a variety of health conditions."

I have occasionally used the interlocked fingers with my hand lightly resting on the head and slowly pulled my hands apart, massaging the top of the skull. Other light massages in the bone above and the upper neck muscles are located at the skull's base, mainly as a de-stressor, usually on either side of the spine.

Sometimes I use a thumb and forefinger pinch over the side neck muscles.

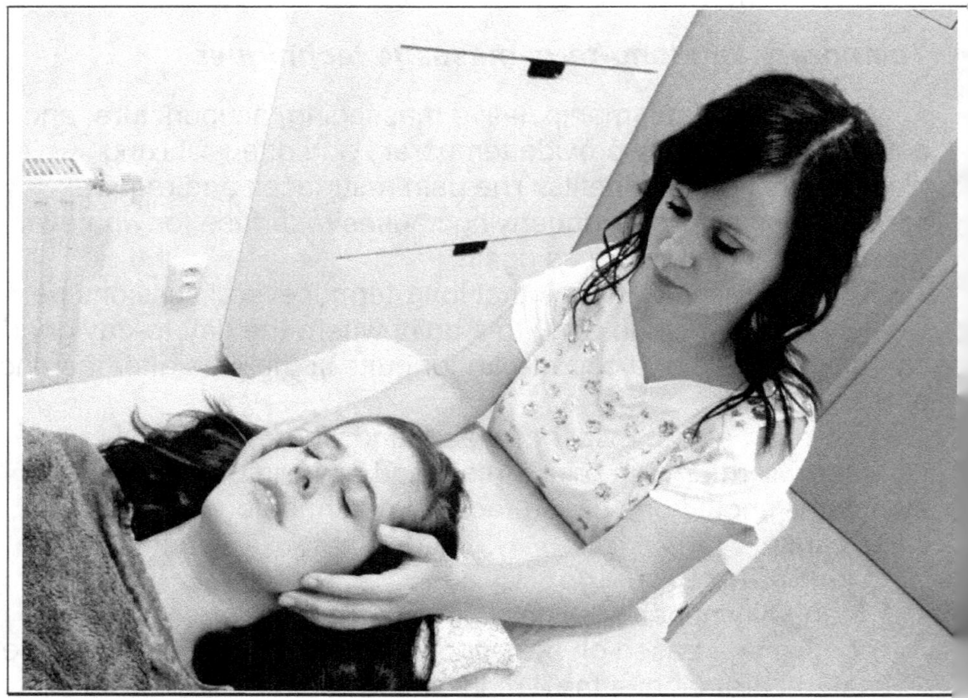

As per the above, I have massaged the temples to alleviate headaches and jaw juncture to loosen my locked, indrawn lower and other's jaw aches.

Chapter 8: Touch for Health

As I mentioned earlier, I would give everyone I healed a hug after each healing in the Spiritualist Church. It was simply to assure them on an animal level with a healing touch.

More than a dozen healers, including myself, took and held the patient's hands to comfort them and convey our sincerity, compassion, and love.

Chapter 9: Deep Breathing Techniques

Yogic Breathing-Pranayama

I, personally, have tried and successfully used both yogic breathing and rebirthing.

Yogic breathing entails the total inflation and deflation of the lungs. The steps in this process are to inflate the lower lung section, thus extending the stomach, fill the mid-chest level fully and then complete with a last movement of the shoulders upwards, thus filling the lungs.

Once filled, hold the breath for a short while and then reverse the process allowing the shoulders to drop, the chest to deflate, and the stomach to return to normal.

Continue for a brief time and cease if you become dizzy.

The above picture shows the hand placement on the stomach and chest. This positioning is helpful as one can feel these areas expand and contract as one breathes; therefore, you can regulate and assess complete deep breathing.

Rebirthing breathwork

I had two sessions with a rebirther. The session involved lying on the floor, cosy and warm, a Duna covering me to my throat region while I did deep, slow breathing. He beat on the drum in the second session and observed only, otherwise no input.

In the first session, I had gone into laboured, heavy breathing towards the end and, according to him, had exhaled putrid smelly air during this. So that indicated the body's natural response to trauma with heavy breathing. It also indicated my not fully inhaling, exhaling, and allowing air to allow smell-inducing bacteria to grow.

The reason for the laboured breathing was: early into the first session, I found myself screaming in a WW2 bomber on fire, nose-diving towards the ground. I believe somewhere in China, however, coming out before dying there.

This pain-filled face rose from me in the second session and exited from my head. Over the next few days, I became increasingly tired and exhausted. It was only after thinking that I may have frightened my spirit out of my body by trying to remember an even more frightening event and wishing for me to return that I reversed the exhausted feeling within hours.

Abnormal reactive, quick short breaths not associated with my meditation practice or the above sessions self-initiate whenever I get close to or touch traumatic memories.

On 5 or 6 occasions, when overwhelmed by emotions, I have begun rapid, deep breathing for up to several minutes. This action aids in riding the emotional turmoil. It takes the edge off, allowing me to return to normal.

The emotion related to this is claustrophobia, initiated whenever someone was trapped in a small, enclosed space or pipe on the screen. The problem surfaced in my mid to late sixties. After those very jittery screen content triggers with forced walkouts, I was not maintaining composure when seeing this. It is now becoming mild to non-existent again. Hopefully, I have breathed it out of me the way others did in a rebirthing book I've read.

Chapter 10: Other Physical bodily reactions encountered

Hearing: In my twenties, when I was meditating, all I heard were the sounds around me. In my thirties, I heard a whistling sound but very faintly. In the forties, the sound grew louder; on two occasions, it turned into a high-pitched shriek.

Over the next 30 years, this high-pitched whistle has intensified and. is now heard whenever it is quiet. Currently, the intensity is just below the roar level.

Another sound awareness increase happened while I was enjoying a float tank session. I could hear music playing three rooms away, over and above the sound of water lapping and a pump flowing.

This sensitivity reminded me of the Kung Fu series where the expert berates his pupil when he can't hear the sound of the cricket many feet away.

The two experiences, however, are different—the first is due to our awareness of the current flowing through our nerves and minds. The acoustic hypersensitivity moments relate to my brain' electric output peaking during two superconscious states. The increase intensifies the decibel range into the ultrasonic with little to no detriment other than a rushed time sense effect.

It relates to hearing ultrasonics without the usual detrimental associated symptoms, headaches and dizziness. The second type: hearing minute soft sounds far away, has more to do with the mind's ability to sort data, even minuscule sounds.

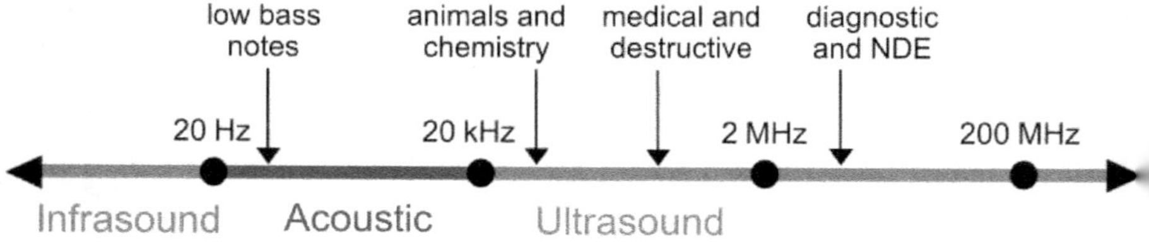

I did a sound test in October 2022, and at 71, I am still in the excellent hearing range, just off 20000htz. However, there is a slight time difference between hearing the sound and reacting to and recording the event.

Endurance changes

After decades of searching, one of the abilities you find is the body's coping mechanism, which is now underutilised in today's socio-economic climate.

Once upon a time, yogis discovered incredible body endurance-breaking miracles through their training regimen. Stories of men buried for months (India), monks able to traverse hundreds of kilometres without breaks via trances (Tibet) and in China, able to make their bodies impervious to swords and clubs.

I can testify to my body's ability to cool down by several degrees in summer and retain that coolness allowing me to fall asleep quickly. In my forties, my body's reaction was the formation of thousands of goosebumps on arms and legs. I believe I can concur with the ability to reduce our need for oxygen, spoken of in several articles and mentioned in books I have read.

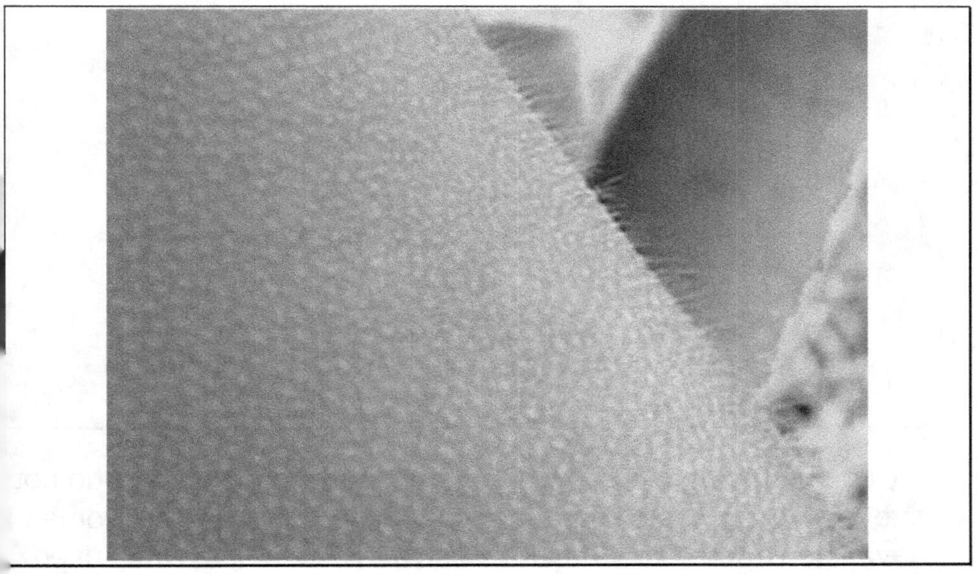

During 2021 in my meditative void mind meditation states, I noticed my breathing becoming negligible and, for a fleeting time, non-existent. However, I cannot say that for sure as I was too into the meditative void mind state to notice. As my eyes became dissociated and I started seeing two of the same image after this, I opted not to try it again.

2022 The reverse cold manifested last and this year as my body has warmed. This warming is consistent with one recent female Christian saint's records. The only negative to this temperature change is that the cooling offset has and is taking longer to achieve.

Stress

Stress can be felt in muscle tones and produce such effects as high blood pressure, indigestion, muscle and bone aches and many other recordable effects. The website listed can provide some 50, https://www.stress.org/stress-effects

This little drawing gives helpful hints on how to relieve it.

My comments on the above not mentioned elsewhere are do not stress on goal meets compared to goal sets. Four of the women I have known who had been in abusive relationships overly used the talk to a friend. So be gentle in your response when they

repeat their lives to you sixty or more times. Repeating in the same order usually means they're not lying about what happened to them. Liars can't keep the repetition up correctly.

As to sleeping better, I know how much it can affect you health-wise when one doesn't, so take time out if you need it. My last year and a half of being a carer for my father almost broke me after only getting 2-3 hours of undisturbed sleep per night.

Chapter 11: Purification Rituals

Purification rituals have been part of the spiritual journey for thousands of years. The Americas, Europe, the Middle East, and the East: India to Japan all had them.

Water in liquid form

John baptises Jesus.

Four religions use water as a purifying agent, e.g., the baptism ceremony in the Christian both as above and more effective as total immersion, various purification rites in the Jewish and Muslim faith, and water rituals regarding Mother Ganges in India.

Tamil purification

Like the Christians and the saint's processions to the sea, the Indians take their Gods to the Ganges.

Does the purification with water work? Putting all the religious connotations aside, it does both the hot and cold-water ones. By the way, it's the total immersion, not the dab of a small cup over the head and the anointing with oil, which does nothing.

I shower hot in winter and cold in summer and feel better for it, cleansed of the physical and lower energy grime, not sin.

Water as steam

Steam has been used by many cultures historically. These being. The Norse, North American Indians and even the Romans with their bathhouses. Although this technique, I would place more in the ascetic's practises as it strains the limits of our bodies.

It certainly opens the pores, and sweating is good for the skin, heart, general well-being, pain, toxin reduction, aids cancer patient treatment, reduces inflammation, improves memory, assists in diabetes and improves physical fitness. Dry saunas are better than humid ones, although, for chest complaints, I find a steam and eucalyptus inhalation most helpful.

For further information, visit this site 10 Sauna Benefits for Your Health & Wellness (foodrevolution.org)

Chapter 12: Asceticism and Penance

Asceticism is defined as: "a severe self-deprivation for ethical, religious, or intellectual ends."

There is a vast spectrum in this technique. At the lower end is fasting for one day or more, a practice performed by people worldwide, regardless of their religious background.

The high-end spectrum sometimes almost dying due to a fictitious belief. The Buddha below shows his emaciated state following the extreme form of this practice. Milarepa in Tibetan Buddhism and Jesus and Francis of Assisi in the Christian faith harboured similar notions.

It comes from a mistaken belief that refraining from pleasures and attempting to cleanse their body with this practice progresses their spiritual advancement.

Buddha and Milarepa found this path useless after almost dying from starvation. This practice does not work.

Admittedly I have read dozens of posts on Facebook praising this fasting act and detailing the benefits thereof. However, here are things to look out for. Fasting can cause dehydration, so kee fluids up. Any weight loss is just fluid; this will return when you stop the fast. Other negatives are increased stress levels and sleep disruption leading to headaches and heartburn as the acid in your stomach starts affecting the lining.

Another problem is that when the body burns the fat we have stored, it also releases toxins in that fat, which can cause headaches and fatigue. Dani's friend, who had been obese, lost significant weight and died from a heart attack. I suspect, and there is undoubtedly internet verification, that this sudden weight loss can cause it.

The benefits include immune increases as the body destroys damaged cells and replaces those destroyed with new ones, detoxification and a fasting high.

Please be aware the body begins to break down muscle tissue instead of fat initially.

Penance

Definition: "punishment inflicted on oneself as an outward expression of repentance for wrongdoing:"

The lightest penance is reciting prayers after confession; intermediate is the Hindu lying on rocks, worst I've read is self-flagellation and mimicry of the wounds of Christ.

Efficacy of the above disciplines.

The only benefit would be body cleansing via fasting, as a water diet can flush the body. Fasting is not a weight-loss regime.

Starving or beating yourself merely adds to the trauma already in your body and in no way cleanses you.

Differences

Buddha and Milarepa tried to cut out food, and it was only luck that someone found them and gave them nutritious food, which made them realise the error of their thinking.

Christ spent 40 days in the desert; some Native Americans underwent extremely painful rituals to attain a state where visions came.

Chapter 13: Posture

Problems related to posture can include respiratory imbalances, muscular strains, bone misplacement and heartburn.

On the spiritual side, good posture is the automatic state of repose in deep meditation, i.e. as the mind returns to rest, the body adopts the correct posture I've found. It also allows deep unrestricted breathing.

There are also posture poses in yoga.

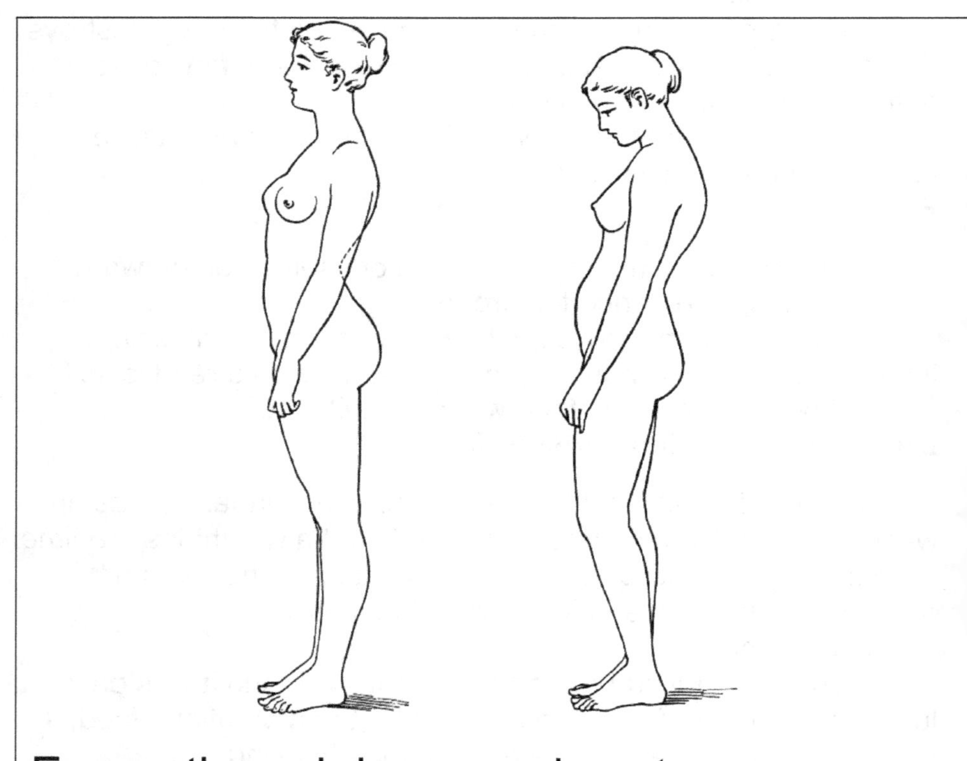

Energetic and depressed posture.

Chapter 14: Pointers for practitioners and patients.

While performing both massage and acupuncture involve the patient in the process. By involve, I mean while you are performing the treatment, have them note the following: with massage, pain spots and where they are felt. During acupuncture, any linked and associated pain spots. Have them quickly inform you if the treatment is too painful using a safe word. Then switch from the treatment to support if they go into full release.

If anything emotional surfaces, have them write it down for later reference.

With rebirthing and deep breathing, note changes in body posture and breathing rate. If the breathing rate becomes excessively fast, check the patient's condition before continuing. The patient should release gradually rather than all in one hit.

I cannot impress the observation and support function, especially if the patient undergoes a traumatic release.

Remember to get them to breathe out of the trauma episode should it occur and you can't stop it normally.

Chapter 15: Food in the Spiritual Equation

Our physical body is a biological and electrical organism. As such, it requires food to grow, stay healthy, and obtain sustenance. Other than to say the fresher or the more alive and natural the food is, the better it is for you, I leave it to you to decide whatever you are comfortable eating. I prefer organically home-grown produce because it tastes better, and I enjoy gardening.

Eating raw meat is the exception; I prefer it cooked, although I will probably need to try a few more sushi dishes before I sometimes go the other way. Raw chicken is a no-no, given all the germs that are included in the bird nowadays. Moderation in all things is a good guideline.

I tried a salmon sushi takeaway, and although it was filling for me, one slight salty, salmon gingery taste was overpowered by the rice after the first few bites.

I had several run-ins with toxic gases, and let me say that it is incredible that although it left me chemically sensitised to organic carbon solvents, it awoke my innate sense of food choice.

The injury removed some of the blockages I had put up, as my body knew what could help me recover. It also automatically directed me to healing food sources, e.g. (Vegemite, fresh salads and anti-inflammatories (Ibuprofen), until my stomach started having problems).

So, if you occasionally find yourself particularly drawn to something not in the supposedly dangerous category, it could very well be you need it, or you're pregnant. This intuitive food need is pronounced during pregnancy.

Do not deny your innate intuitive side. My Polish friend used to devour her chocolate because it was a substitute pleasure for traditional family life. Let us say it was eaten entirely on the same day given or bought. Better be happy than sad, I always say.

As the old teachers and gurus drilled a healthy body necessity into their pupils, I find that a good gardening pursuit in my backyard fulfils this for me.

Chapter 16: Aftereffects of Spiritual Releases

The number of times I have heard, "I've just had a release, and I now feel the worse for it." on Facebook is phenomenal. Unfortunately, spiritual releases do have adverse side effects. Every time I noticed a tripped indicator of having had a spiritual awareness increase, my body had a detrimental effect lasting between one and two to 4 days.

The correlation between spiritual awareness increases and the length of feeling like you have gotten or are getting over the flu are proportional to each other.

Yes, spiritual changes release toxins stored in our bodies, giving us flu-like symptoms, like lethargy and muscular pain. These symptoms only last a couple of days compared to viral infections that linger and have more varied and changing symptoms.

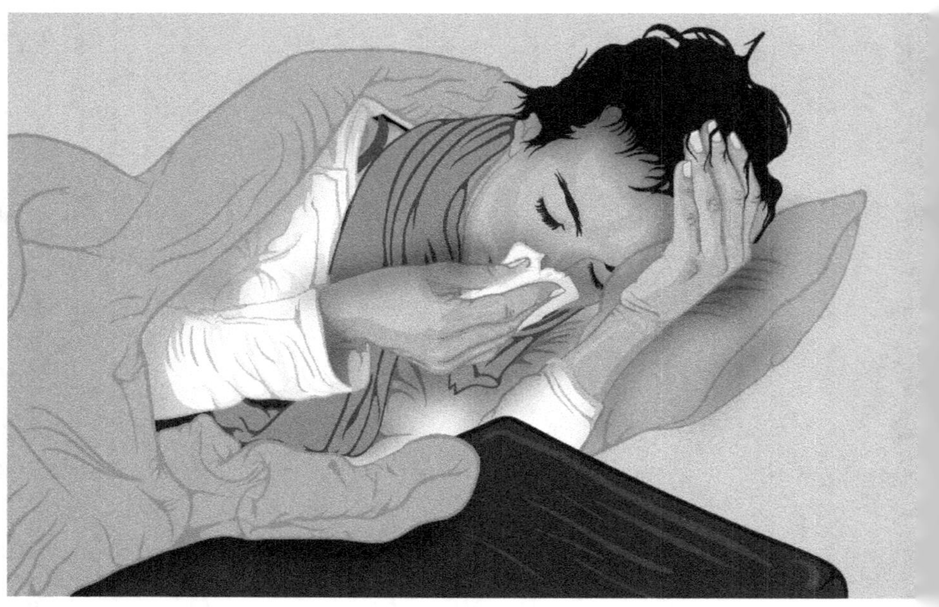

Summary

I have read many posts on the internet and in books and have been told of the fantastic spiritual breakthroughs by using yoga, rebirthing, and acupuncture separately. I have only benefitted from the pain relief from acupuncture, stress relief and pleasure from the massage, and the unexpected ejection of spirit and a past life memory using rebirthing. None of which I considered improved me spiritually.

In my massage on people requesting healing, I used only one, sometimes two methods rarely. Again, no great benefits other than those stated above for me.

While using all three on my rescue lady in my sixties, I will admit she went from having a highly stressed, taught body and emotionally reactive mental state to one capable of returning to work after years away on worker's compensation. She was then promoted after several months back in the workforce and remained stable for a year.

From this perspective, the overall treatments stabilised her and allowed her coping mechanism to succeed. She maintained stability until another work injury in a high-pressure workplace destabilised her.

From a stabilising perspective, all physical body remedial options work and allow us to move on to the other areas more easily. I suspect this toning and body release was the main reason; historically, maintaining a healthy body was part of the spiritual routine.

Although the following picture is broken down into separate segments of the body system, know that working on even only one will affect all the others also. There is a symbiotic relationship between all parts of your body, physical and electrical.

Human Body Organ Systems

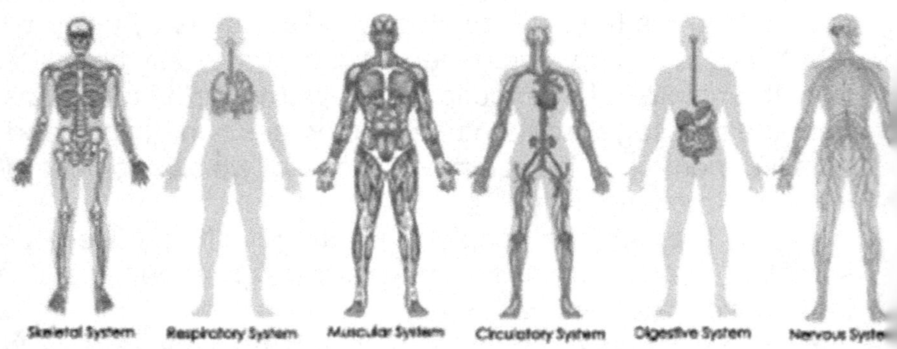

Bibliography
Wikipedia

Page 10: Kriya's definition

Page 14: wikipedia/commons/d/d5/Akmanthor.jpg

Page 17: File: Yang-single (restoration).jpg

Page 17: File: Shi DeRu and Shi DeYang.jpg

Page 18: File: Hupa Sweat House.jpg

Page 20: 1921px Chinese meridians

Page 22: Acupuncture needles

Page 23: Acupressure

Page 24: File: Cupping set, London, England Welcomed L0057395.jpg

Page 25: File: Skeletal muscles homo sapiens.JPG

Page 26: File:Kiropraktisk ledd-korreksjon av rygg.jpg

Page 26: File: Activator II adjustment instrument.png

Page 31: TarcisioTS File: Foot Chart1 small.png

Page 32: Arbay File: Reflexology of the Hand.JPG

Page 33: Lymphatic therapy description

Page 33: Craniosacral massage

Page 34: File:Kraniosakrální terapie - biodynamika.jpg

Page 42: John baptising Jesus

Page 38: File: Ultrasound range diagram.svg

Page 39: Goosebumps photo

Page 42: Tamil water purification ceremony.
https://www.flickr.com/people/clodreno/

Page 43: Ganesha purification ceremony.

Page 44: Siddhartha Fasting Gautama Buddha.jpg
https://www.flickr.com/people/90664717@N00

Page 46: File:Gutehaltung desKorbersSchlechteHaltung desKorpers.gif

Page 48: File: a green salad

Page 50: File: A lady suffering from the Common Cold.png

Shutterstock subscription paid

Page 5: 1694225173

Page 12: 1979679575

Page 15: 326069972

Page 16: 561314125

Page 19: 686734900

Page 28: 4099088751

Page 29: 510620557
Page 30: 2059171823
Page 30: 1799310655
Page 32: 21477036659
Page 35: 1155348268
Page 36: 2183284585
Page 40: 1221970162
Page 52: 638539111

Page 10 My photo Stomach kriya breaks meditation

Page 33: https://www.healthsolutions.shop/index

Other Publications

The Bio-electric, Prana, Kundalini, Reiki, Chi, Sha Man's Shaman Ways (autobiography and instructional manual)

Cancer: The Proactive Spiritual Assist Method

UFO's and Spaceship Gods

Lament of a Paedophile Satanist's still surviving Ex-Wife. Compendium of three poems

God Sinned Greatly: Why Couldn't We Sin Slightly

The Great God Question. Does he or she exist.

Meditation: My Methods of Reintegrating Mind and Body

Depression: The Spiritual Ways To Clear The Fog

Baptism by Water. Baptism with Fire

Barred from the Temple

The Reality Bubble

Books assisted via co-writing, editing, illustrating and publishing

His Pact with the Devil

The Perils of Pauline, er Dani

Compendium of Paranormal Experiences of Dani Morena

S.S.S. Spiders

The Handbook for Mothers that do too much

Song lyrics

Ridiculous

Webpage and contact

Contact: mahaete@gmail.com

Website Mahaete.com.